THE GHOST ORCHID

POETRY

No Continuing City
An Exploded View
Man Lying on a Wall
The Echo Gate
Selected Poems
Poems 1963–1983
Gorse Fires

AUTOBIOGRAPHY

Tuppenny Stung

AS EDITOR

Causeway: The Arts in Ulster
Under the Moon, Over the Stars: Children's Poetry
Further Reminiscences: Paul Henry
Selected Poems: Louis MacNeice
Poems: W.R. Rodgers

To Susie

The Ghost Orchid

MICHAEL LONGLEY

Warm wishes
Michael Longley
Sept 97

WAKE FOREST
UNIVERSITY
PRESS

Wake Forest University Press
This book is for sale only in North America.
Poems copyright by Michael Longley
All rights reserved.
For permission, required to reprint or
broadcast more than several lines, write to:
Wake Forest University Press,
P.O. Box 7333
Winston-Salem, NC 27109
Typeset in Bembo
Printed by Thomson-Shore
LC Card no. 95-62042
ISBN 0-926390-72-1
(paperback)
ISBN 0-916390-73-X
(clothbound)

For John & Janet

You walked with me among water mint
And bog myrtle when I was tongue-tied:
When I shouted at the ferny cliff
You adopted my echo like a child.

CONTENTS

FORM

Trying to tell it all to you and cover everything
Is like awakening from its grassy form the hare:
In that make-shift shelter your hand, then my hand
Mislays the hare and the warmth it leaves behind.

AUTUMN LADY'S TRESSES

How does the solitary swan on Dooaghtry Lake
Who knows all about the otter as a glimmer
Among reeds, as water unravelling, as watery
Corridors into the water, a sudden face,
Receive through the huge silence of sand-dunes
Signals from the otters' rock at Allaran Point
About another otter, the same otter, folding
Sunlight into the combers like brown kelp,
Or the dolphins whose waves within waves propel
You and me along the strand like young lovers,
Or the aftermath of lit thistledown, peacock
Butterflies above marram grass, lady's tresses
That wind into their spirals of white flowers
Cowrie shells for decorating your sandy hair?

WATERCOLOUR
for Jeffrey Morgan

Between a chicken's wishbone on the mantelpiece
And, on the window sill, a dolphin's skull, I sit,
My pullover a continuation of the lazy-beds
You study through the window, my shirt a running
Together of earth-colours, wintry grasses, bracken
Painted with your favourite brush – goose-quill and sable
From a hundred years ago – and with water:
One drop too many and the whole thing disintegrates.
In this humidity your watercolour will never dry.

GRETTA BOWEN'S EMENDATIONS

Eighty when she first created pictures, Gretta Bowen
Postponed the finishing touches, and then in her nineties
Emended her world by painting on the glass that covered
Children's games, fairgrounds, swans on a pond, interiors
Not brush-strokes to erase her studious reflection
But additional leaves and feathers falling on to ice.

SITTING FOR EDDIE
in memory of Edward McGuire

I had suggested a spray of beech leaves behind me
Or a frieze of birds – bittern, lapwing, chough –
Or a single carline-thistle representing flowers
Pressed between pages, stuffed birds behind glass, our
Still lives, Eddie's and mine, feathers and petals
That get into the picture like noises-off, long
Distance calls in the small hours, crazed arguments
About the colour of my eyes – his strange mistake –
Jazz to relax me, in an enormous magnifying
Glass our eyes out of all proportion, likenesses
And the trundle of castors under a skylight,
His gambler's eye-shield, the colours of the rainbow,
Me turning into a still life whose eyes are blue.

AFTER HORACE

We postmodernists can live with that human head
Stuck on a horse's neck, or the plastering of multi-
Coloured feathers over the limbs of assorted animals
(So that what began on top as a gorgeous woman
Tapers off cleverly into the tail of a black fish).

Since our fertile imaginations cannot make head
Or tail of anything, wild things interbreed with tame,
Snakes with birds, lambs with tigers. If a retired sailor
Commissions a picture of the shipwreck he survived,
We give him a cypress-tree because we can draw that.

To relieve the boredom we introduce to the woods
A dolphin, a wild boar to the waves. Ultimate post-
Modernists even in the ceramics department we
May have a vase in mind when we start, or a wine-jug,
But, look, as the wheel goes round, it ends up as a po.

THE MAD POET

When someone's afflicted with the itchy nirls
Or jaundice or religious fundamentalism,
You don't play tig with him: ditto the mad poet,
Head in the air, burping pomes, dootering about:

And if, like a wildfowler gawking at blackbirds,
He cope-carlies into a waterhole or heugh
And gulders 'Hi! dear readers! Help!' – do not
Swing him a life-line: sling him a deafie instead.

How do you know he isn't cowping accident-
ally on purpose (and *likes* it down there) just as
That head-the-ball Empedocles a header took
– In hot pursuit of immortality – into Etna?

It's still not clear what hurts him into verse, whether
He pissed on his father's ashes (in the urn) or
Thrappled his muse: at all events he is horn-daft
Like a bear bending the bars of his limitations.

His mad-dog shite has everyone – the poetry-buffs
And the iggerant – shit-scared: he grabbles you, then
He reads you to death, a leech cleeking your skin
Who won't drop off until he is boke-full of blood.

PERDIX

In the wings of that story about the failure of wings
– Broken wings, wings melting, feathers on water, Icarus –
The garrulous partridge crows happily from a sheugh
And claps its wings, a hitherto unheard-of species,
The latest creation, a grim reminder to Daedalus
– Inventor, failure's father – of his apprentice, a boy
Who had as a twelve-year-old the mental capacity
To look at the backbone of a fish and invent the saw
By cutting teeth in a metal blade; to draw conclusions
And a circle with the first compass, two iron limbs,
Arms, legs tied together, geometry's elbow or knee –

Which proved his downfall, for Daedalus grew so jealous
He pushed the prodigy headlong off the Acropolis
And then fibbed about him slipping; but Pallas Athene
Who supports the ingenious, intercepted his fall,
Dressed him in feathers in mid-air and made him a bird,
Intelligence flashing to wing-tip and claw, his name
Passing on to the bird (it is *perdix* in the Greek) –
The partridge that avoids getting airborne and nesting
In tree-tops or on dizzy ledges; that flapping along
At ground level, laying its eggs under hedges, has lost,
Thanks to the memory of that tumble, its head for heights.

ACCORDING TO PYTHAGORAS

When in good time corpses go off and ooze in the heat
Creepy-crawlies breed in them. Bury your prize bull
(A well-known experiment) – and from the putrid guts
Swarm flower-crazy bees, industrious country-types
Working hard, as did their host, with harvest in mind.
An interred war-horse produces hornets. Remove
A shore-crab's hollow claw, lay it to rest: the result
Is a scorpion charging with its tail bent like a hook.
Worms cosy in cocoons of white thread grow into
Butterflies, souls of the dead. Any farmer knows that.

Germs in mud generate green frogs: legless at first
They soon sprout swimming and jumping equipment.
A she-bear's cub is a lump of meat whose stumpy
Non-legs she licks into shape in her own image.
The honey-bees' larvae hatched in those waxy hexagons
Only get feet and wings later on. That's obvious.
Think of peacocks, eagles, doves, the bird-family
As a whole, all starting inside eggs: hard to believe.
There's a theory that in the grave the backbone rots
Away and the spinal cord turns into a snake.

The fundamental interconnectedness of all things
Is incredible enough, but did you know that
Hyenas change sex? The female mounted by a male
Just minutes before, becomes a male herself. Then
There's the chameleon that feeds off wind and air
And takes the colour of whatever it's standing on.
Air transforms lynxes' urine into stones and hardens
Coral, that softly swaying underwater plant.
I could go on and on with these scientific facts.
If it wasn't so late I'd tell you a whole lot more.

KESTREL

Because an electric pylon was the kestrel's perch
I wanted her to scan the motorway's long acre
And the tarmac and grassy patches at the airport
And undress her prey in the sky and beat the air
Above grasshopper and skylark as the wind-fucker.

OASIS

Because the rain fell over a thousand years ago
The sand-grouse does not bury his head like the skink
That swims in the sand – more an eddy than a ripple –
But mounts his ancient reflection and then with wet
Feathers breastfeeds his chicks and irrigates the zenith.

ICICLE

Though the caddis-fly does something similar with
    hailstones
Knitting them into a waistcoat for her shivering larva,
The ants carry snowflakes inside their nest to make an
    icicle
Which will satisfy the huge queen and her ignorant grubs
And prove that the melting snowman was somebody's
    child.

SHE-WOLF

Fingers and toes, a tail wagging,
And there in the middle
Rome like a sore belly-button
Peeps out from the huddle.

She licks Romulus and Remus
The moment they piddle,
Her cold nose tickling the heads
That nod off and nuddle.

HIPPOMANES

Randiest of all, taking in their stride mountains
And rapids for sex, biting your hand off, mares,
Kindled in springtime, gonads ablaze, silhouetted
On a cliff where they turn as one to face the wind,
Snuffle the air and often – not a stallion in sight –
Are impregnated:
                 they have been ridden by the wind
And clatter down rocky scree to the valley floor
And scatter, not to the east and sunrise, but south
Where the wind sheds tears from a sky in mourning
And a slippery liquid oozes from their quims,
Hippomanes no less, collected by jealous step-
Mothers and blended with herbs and mumbo-jumbo.

SHEELA-NA-GIG

She pulls her vulva apart for everyone to look at,
Not just for me, a stonemason deflowering stone.
She behaves thus above the church door at Kilnaboy
Where the orchids have borrowed her cunty petals.
A proper libation would be sperm and rainwater.
Ivy grows over her forehead, wall-rue at her feet.

SPIDERWOMAN

Arachne starts with Ovid and finishes with me.

Her hair falls out and the ears and nostrils disappear
From her contracting face, her body minuscule, thin
Fingers clinging to her sides by way of legs, the rest
All stomach, from which she manufactures gossamer
And so keeps up her former trade, weaver, spider

Enticing the eight eyes of my imagination
To make love on her lethal doily, to dangle sperm
Like teardrops from an eyelash, massage it into her
While I avoid the spinnerets – navel, vulva, bum –
And the widening smile behind her embroidery.

She wears our babies like brooches on her abdomen.

A FLOWERING

Now that my body grows woman-like I look at men
As two or three women have looked at me, then hide
Among Ovid's lovely casualties – all that blood
Colouring the grass and changing into flowers, purple,
Lily-shaped, wild hyacinth upon whose petals
We doodled our lugubrious initials, they and I,
Blood dosed with honey, tumescent, effervescent
– Clean bubbles in yellow mud – creating in an hour
My own son's beauty, the truthfulness of my nipples,
Petals that will not last long, that hang on and no more,
Youth and its flower named after the wind, anemone.

ROSEMARY

She stood among the nasturtiums on a rubbish dump
And laid on the ground her handkerchief-full of
    blackberries
And lifted her skirt and moistened the hem with spittle
And dabbed the purple away from the corners of my
    mouth.

IVORY & WATER

If as a lonely bachelor who disapproves of women
You carve the perfect specimen out of snow-white ivory
And fall in love with your masterpiece and make love
    to her
(Or try to) stroking, fondling, whispering, kissing,
    nervous
In case you bruise ivory like flesh with prodding fingers,
And bring sea-shells, shiny pebbles, song-birds,
    colourful wild
Flowers, amber-beads, orchids, beach-balls as her presents,
And put real women's clothes, wedding rings, ear-rings,
    long
Necklaces, a brassière on the statue, then undress her
And lay her in your bed, her head on the feathery pillows
As if to sleep like a girlfriend, your dream may come true
And she warms and softens and you are kissing actual lips
And she blushes as she takes you in, the light of her eyes,
And her veins pulse under your thumb at the end of
    the dream
When she breaks out in a cold sweat that trickles into pools
And drips from her hair dissolving it and her fingers
    and toes,
Watering down her wrists, shoulders, rib-cage, breasts
    until
There is nothing left of her for anyone to hug or hold.

MR. 10½
after Robert Mapplethorpe

When he lays out as on a market stall or altar
His penis and testicles in thanksgiving and for sale,
I find myself considering his first months in the womb
As a wee girl, and I substitute for his two plums
Plum-blossom, for his cucumber a yellowy flower.

MASSIVE LOVERS
after Katsushika Hokusai

I was the philosopher watching a pair of butterflies
Until massive lovers exposed my peedy and grey hairs –
His cock a gate-post, rain running off the glans,
    snow-broth
And the shriek of silk, hair-pins along the loney – and I
Became the pearl-diver hugged and sucked by octopuses.

A GIFT OF BOXES

I

Rice grains between my chopsticks remind you of
    a flower.
I want to wash the hagi petals in my bowl, then balance
Before your lips an offering of crabs' brains on a shiso leaf
Which looks like a nettle from Ireland but does not sting.

II

We are completely out of proportion in the tea-house
Until we arrange around a single earthenware bowl
Ourselves, the one life, one meeting, a ribbon of water
And these makeshift ideograms of wet leaves, green tea.

III

You make a gift of boxes by putting boxes inside
Boxes, each one containing the Japanese air you breathe,
More and more of it in diminishing boxes, smallness
Condensing in the end to two boxes the size of tears.

IV

They have planted stones in the stone garden. If I sit still
The stones will take root in my imagination and grow.
You retire behind the fifteenth stone which I cannot see.
Whatever happens to a stone becomes its life, its flower.

A GRAIN OF RICE

Wrap my poem around your chopsticks to keep them
    clean.
I hardly know you. I do not want you to die. Our names
Fit on to a grain of rice like Hokusai's two sparrows,
Or else, like the praying mantis and the yellow butterfly,
We are a crowd in the garden where nothing grows but
    stones.
I do not understand the characters: sunlight through leaves,
An ivy pattern like fingers caressing a bowl, your face
In splinters where a carp kisses the moon, the waterfall
Up which its fins will spiral out of sight and into the sky.
Wrap my poem around your chopsticks to keep them
    clean.
Does it mean I shall not have taken one kiss for ever?
Your unimaginable breasts become the silk-worm's shrine.

CHINESE OBJECTS

I

The length of white silk I selected
Immaculate as the crust on snow
Was cut in the shape of happiness,
Round as the moon in starry skies.
In and out of her sleeve it slides
Rustling up its own cool weather.
I worry that when autumn comes
And blows away this heatwave,
She will toss the fan into a box
Half way through our love affair.

II

When the water-gourd that dangles
Light as a single leaf from the tree
Goes clickety-clack in the breeze
So that bed-sounds and love-making
Get into my dream, in my dream
I throw it away, for the world
Is not so big, the gourd so small:
They are objects outside my body
That get in the way of sleep.

CHINESE WHISPERS

'From the south it's a long way
With wildfowlers lying in wait.
How many geese will make it
Through the mist, no–one can say.'

'Don't shoot the last to migrate
From the south: let them fly north.
If you do shoot, shoot them both,
So they won't have to separate.'

A PAIR OF SHOES

Who stole my shoes from the Garden of Ryoan–ji?
Have they come near you in Tokyo or Nagoya
Or Takayama? Fifteen rocks make up the landscape
We borrow, faraway places in gravelly sea.

THE SHIP OF THE WIND
after the Dutch

I

The oars, heavy with seaweed, at rest in humid mists;
The home-made sail folded at the edge of the ocean;
And over their unassuming faces, lamp-light
That after a day's work is the soul of evening.

They are eating. Food spicy with peace and friendship;
The child's sleepy happiness soothing the cabin;
The lentils and the fish and the rose-pink radishes;
The mother's breasts rising and falling as she breathes.

II

The sun and the sea have erupted, sheet-lightning,
Fans of fire and silk;
Along the blue mountains of morning
The wind grazes like a gazelle.

I stroll between fountains of light,
Around watery, radiant piazzas
With a fair-haired woman who is singing
In clear tones to the everlasting ocean

This lighthearted air that beguiles me:

'The ship of the wind lies ready for our journey,
The sun and the moon are snow-white roses,
Morning and night are two blue sailors –
We shall return to Paradise.'

BAUCIS & PHILEMON
for Brian & Denise Ferran

In the Phrygian hills an oak tree grows beside a lime tree
And a low wall encloses them. Not far away lies bogland.
I have seen the spot myself. It should convince you
– If you need to be convinced – that the power of heaven
Is limitless, that whatever the gods desire gets done.

Where a drowned valley makes a sanctuary for water birds
(Divers, coots), a whole community used to plough – until
Jupiter brought Mercury without his wand or wings.
Disguised as humans, they knocked at a thousand houses
Looking for lodgings. A thousand houses slammed the
    door.

But one house took them in, a cottage thatched with straw
And reeds from the bog. Baucis and Philemon, a kindly
Old couple, had been married there when they were young
And, growing old together there, found peace of mind
By owning up to their poverty and making light of it.

Pointless to look for masters or servants here because
Wife and husband served and ruled the household equally.
So, when these sky-dwellers appeared at their
    cottage-home
Stooping under the low door to get in, the old man
Brought them stools to sit on, the old woman cushions.

She raked the warm ashes to one side and fanned into life
Yesterday's embers which she fed with leaves and
    dry bark,
The breath from her old body puffing them into flames.
She hoked around in the roof-space for twigs
    and firewood,
Broke them up and poked the kindling under her skillet.

She took the cabbage which Philemon had brought her
From the garden plot, and lopped off the outer leaves. He
Lowered a flitch of smoked bacon from the sooty rafters
And carved a reasonable helping from their precious pork
Which he simmered in bubbling water to make a stew.

They chatted to pass the time for their hungry visitors
And poured into a beechwood bucket dangling from
    its peg
Warm water so that the immortals might freshen up.
Over a sofa, its feet and frame carved out of willow,
Drooped a mattress lumpy with sedge-grass from the
    river.

On this they spread a coverlet, and the gods sat down.
The old woman tucked up her skirts and with shaky hands
Placed the table in front of them. Because one leg
    was short
She improvised a wedge and made the surface level
Before wiping it over with a sprig of water-mint.

She put on the table speckly olives and wild cherries
Pickled in wine, endives, radishes, cottage-cheese and eggs
Gently cooked in cooling ashes, all served on crockery.
Next, she produced the hand-decorated wine-jug
And beechwood cups polished inside with yellow wax.

In no time meat arrived from the fireplace piping hot
And the wine, a rough and ready vintage, went the rounds
Until they cleared the table for a second course – nuts
And figs and wrinkly dates, plums and sweet-smelling
    apples
In a wicker basket, purple grapes fresh from the vines.

The centrepiece was a honeycomb oozing clear honey,
And, over everything, the circle of convivial faces
And the bustle of hospitality. And then the hosts
Noticed that the wine jug, as soon as it was emptied,
Filled itself up again – an inexhaustible supply.

This looked like a miracle to Philemon and Baucis
Who, waving their hands about as if in prayer or shock,
Apologised for their home-cooking and simple recipes.
They had just one gander, guardian of the small-holding,
Whom they wanted to sacrifice for the divinities.

But he was too nippy for them and flapped out of danger
Into the immortals' arms. 'Don't kill the goose!' they
    thundered.
'We're gods. Your tightfisted neighbours are about to get
What they deserve. You two are granted immunity.
Abandon your home and climb the mountainside with us.'

Unsteady on their walking-sticks they struggled up
    the steep
Slope and glancing back, a stone's throw from the top,
    they saw
The townland flooded, with just their homestead high
    and dry.
While they stood flabbergasted, crying out for neighbours,
Their cottage (a squeeze for the two of them) became
    a church.

24

Stone pillars took the place of the home-made wooden
        piles,
The thatching glowed so yellow that the roof looked
        golden,
Filigree transformed the doorway, and marble tiling
Improved the dirt floor. Jupiter spoke like a gentleman:
'Grandpa, if you and your good wife could have one
        wish . . .?'

'May we work as vergers in your chapel, and, since
        our lives
Have been spent together, please may we die together,
The two of us at the one time? I don't want to see
My wife buried or be buried by her.' Their wish came true
And up to the last moment they looked after the chapel.

At the end of their days when they were very old
        and bowed
And living on their memories, outside the chapel door
Baucis who was leafy too watched Philemon sprouting
        leaves.
As tree-tops overgrew their smiles they called in unison
'Goodbye, my dear'. Then the bark knitted and hid
        their lips.

Two trees are grafted together where their two bodies
        stood.
I add my flowers to bouquets in the branches by saying
'Treat those whom God loves as your local gods – a
        blackthorn
Or a standing stone. Take care of caretakers and watch
Over the nightwatchman and the nightwatchman's wife.'

WATER-LILY

I

As if Venus and Betelgeuse had wings
And instead of mountainside or tree-top

Had found the right place for falling stars
And glided to a standstill on the lake . . .

II

after Frederik van Eeden

I love the white water-lily, immaculate,
Unfolding her corolla in daylight.

Rising from the cold sediments of the lake
She has seen the light and then unlocked

Her heart of gold: on the surface at one
With herself, her very own creation.

III

Finding my way by night-lights in the sky
I splash through puddles the size of the moon

To a lake the size of the Milky Way
Which I shall call the water-lily lake.

THE SCISSORS CEREMONY

What they are doing makes their garden feel like a
    big room.
I spy on them through the hedge, through a hundred
    keyholes.
He sits in a deckchair. She leans over him from behind
As though he were a little boy, and clips his fingernails
Into the newspaper he balances between his knees. Her
White hair tickles his white hair. Her breath at his ear
Might be correcting his sums, disclosing the facts of life,
Recalling the other warm cheeks that have hesitated there.
He is not demented or lazy or incapacitated. No,
It is just that she enjoys clipping his fingernails
And scattering them like seeds out of a rattly packet.
Are they growing younger as I walk the length of the
    hedge?
Look! The scissors ceremony is a way of making love!

COUPLET

When I was young I wrote that flowers are very slow
    flames
And you uncovered your breasts often among my images.

LIZARD

So small its brassy hand,
Lightfingered its fingers,
I saw a brooch that you
Could wear next your skin.

I wanted it to curl
Its detachable tail
Under your collar-bone
As though to drink there,

But the moment I moved
It skittered first of all
Between your breasts and then
Over your shoulder.

BLACKBIRD

On our side of the glass
You laid out the blackbird's
Sleepy eyes, its twiggy
Toes, crisp tail-feathers
And its wings wider than
The light from two windows.

CHENAC
for Maurice Hayes

I

Today nothing happens in Chenac except for me
And you in the old bakery Maurice is rebuilding,
Rafters like branches, altar-wide hearth, cobwebby
Cubby-holes where yeast fizzed, bread cooled: our estate
Sweet blackberries and windfalls beside the marguerites;
Our guardians the spider out of the Book of Proverbs
That takes hold with her hands, and is in kings' palaces,
The centipede that shimmies where the cellar will be.

II

On twin pillars in St Martin's church bunches of grapes
And orioles repeat themselves and reach the starry sky
A child painted above the altar; until the bell
Recalls diminutive single sunflowers sprouting here
And there, outcasts that escaped both sowing and harvest;
On the road to Épargnes where you can see our steeple
The buzzard with nowhere to perch but stubbly furrows
Flapping to his mate, a tangle of straw in his talons.

III

Accompanying us indoors before a rain-storm the lizard
Zig-zags into his cranny, who is exceeding wise
And makes his house in the rocks and therefore in
    this house.

PHOENIX

I'll hand to you six duck eggs Orla Murphy gave me
In a beechwood bowl Ted O'Driscoll turned, a nest
Jiggling eggs from Baltimore to Belfast, from friends
You haven't met, a double-yolk inside each shell
Laid by a duck that renovates and begets itself
Inside my head as the phoenix, without grass or corn,
On a strict diet of frankincense and cardamoms,
After five centuries builds with talons and clean beak
In the top branches of a quivering palm his nest,
Lining it with cassia, spikes of nard, cinnamon chips
And yellow myrrh, brooding among the spicy smells
His own death and giving birth to an only child
Who grows up to carry through thin air the heavy nest
– His cradle, his father's coffin – to the sun's city,
In front of the sun's doorway putting his bundle down
As I shall put down the eggs Orla Murphy gave me
In a beechwood bowl Ted O'Driscoll turned for her.

POSEIDON

Standing behind the god Poseidon I can see
Through his buttocks to the scrotum's omega.

When I helped Grandpa George into the bath
The same view led me to my mother and me.

His skin seemed dusted as if by moths' wings,
The creases behind his knees like a little boy's.

The god drops whatever he was brandishing
– Trident or thunderbolt – into the bathwater.

AKROTIRI

Next to the window-frame made out of air, a door
Where ash surrounds and balances a pitcher
As though by itself labour might be mummified
And history left ajar for the water-carrier.

THE DRY CLEANERS
Poem Beginning with a Line of Raymond Carver

That time I tagged along with my dad to the dry cleaners
We bumped into Eurycleia whose afternoon-off it was
And bought her tea and watched her smooth the table-
Cloth and make her plate and doily concentric circles, then
Pick up cake-crumbs with a moistened finger, since to us
There was more to her than jugs and basins, hot water
And cold, bed-linen she tested against her cheek after
The rainy trek from clothes-line to airing cupboard. Once
She carried a lamp across the yard in front of me
And saw me to my bedroom and folded my clothes and
Smoothed them and hung them on a peg by my
    wooden bed
And pulled the door to by its silver handle and drew
Home the bolt with the leather strap and left me alone
Worried but cosy through the night under woolly
    blankets.
Eurycleia the daughter of Ops the son of Peisoner
Took care of me and haunts our wardrobe as the
    plastic bags
My clothes come back from the dry cleaners shrouded in.

A BED OF LEAVES

He climbed to the copse, a conspicuous place near water,
And crawled under two bushes sprouting from one
    stem (olive
And wild olive), a thatch so close neither gale-force winds
Nor sunlight nor cloudbursts could penetrate: it was here
Odysseus snuggled and heaped on his mattress of leaves
An eiderdown of leaves, enough to make a double-bed
In winter, whatever the weather, and smiled to himself
When he saw his bed and stretched out in the middle of it
And let even more of the fallen leaves fall over him:
As when a lonely man on a lonely farm smoors the fire
And hides a turf-sod in the ashes to save an ember,
So was his body in the bed of leaves its own kindling
And sleep settled on him like ashes and closed his eyelids.

SNOW-HOLE

Falling asleep in the snowscape of the big double-bed
I wrap my hand around your hand until they catch fire
And the snow begins to melt and we sink down and
    down,
The fire and ourselves, how many feet below the morning.
Should our fingers burn out at the bottom of the
    snow-hole
Smoke will escape up the glass chimney into the bedroom.

THE EEL-TRAP

I lie awake and my mind goes out to the otter
That might be drowning in the eel-trap:
                            your breathing
Falters as I follow you to the other lake
Below sleep, the brown trout sipping at the stars.

THE KILT

I waken you out of your nightmare as I wakened
My father when he was stabbing a tubby German
Who pleaded and wriggled in the back bedroom.

He had killed him in real life and in real life had killed
Lice by sliding along the pleats a sizzling bayonet
So that his kilt unravelled when he was advancing.

You pick up the stitches and with needle and thread
Accompany him out of the grave and into battle,
Your arms full of material and his nakedness.

BEHIND A CLOUD

I

When my father stumbled over gassy corpses
And challenged the shadow of himself on duck-boards,
A field of turnips had filled with German helmets
And under his feet eyes were looking at the moon.

II

When I heard the storm petrel that walks on tiptoe
Over the waves, pattering the surface, purring
And hiccupping, the moon had gone behind a cloud
And changed the sea into a field full of haycocks.

A PAT OF BUTTER
after Hugo Claus

The doddery English veterans are getting
Fewer, and point out to fewer doddery pals
Hill Sixty, Hill Sixty-one, Poelkapelle.

My dad's ghost rummages for his medals
And joins them for tea after the march-past.
The butter tastes of poppies in these parts.

THE CAMP-FIRES

All night crackling camp-fires boosted their morale
As they dozed in no man's land and the killing fields.
(There are balmy nights – not a breath, constellations
Resplendent in the sky around a dazzling moon –
When a clearance high in the atmosphere unveils
The boundlessness of space, and all the stars are out
Lighting up hill-tops, glens, headlands, vantage
Points like Tonakeera and Allaran where the tide
Turns into Killary, where salmon run from the sea,
Where the shepherd smiles on his luminous townland.
That many camp-fires sparkled in front of Ilium
Between the river and the ships, a thousand fires,
Round each one fifty men relaxing in the fire-light.)
Shuffling next to the chariots, munching shiny oats
And barley, their horses waited for the sunrise.

THE HELMET

When shiny Hector reached out for his son, the wean
Squirmed and buried his head between his nurse's breasts
And howled, terrorised by his father, by flashing bronze
And the nightmarish nodding of the horse-hair crest.

His daddy laughed, his mammy laughed, and his daddy
Took off the helmet and laid it on the ground to gleam,
Then kissed the babbie and dandled him in his arms and
Prayed that his son might grow up bloodier than him.

THE PARTING

He: 'Leave it to the big boys, Andromache.'
'Hector, my darling husband, och, och,' she.

38

CEASEFIRE

I

Put in mind of his own father and moved to tears
Achilles took him by the hand and pushed the old king
Gently away, but Priam curled up at his feet and
Wept with him until their sadness filled the building.

II

Taking Hector's corpse into his own hands Achilles
Made sure it was washed and, for the old king's sake,
Laid out in uniform, ready for Priam to carry
Wrapped like a present home to Troy at daybreak.

III

When they had eaten together, it pleased them both
To stare at each other's beauty as lovers might,
Achilles built like a god, Priam good–looking still
And full of conversation, who earlier had sighed:

IV

'I get down on my knees and do what must be done
And kiss Achilles' hand, the killer of my son.'

POPPIES

I

Some people tried to stop other people wearing poppies
And ripped them from lapels as though uprooting poppies
From Flanders fields, but the others hid inside their poppies
Razor blades and added to their poppies more red poppies.

II

In Royal Avenue they tossed in the air with so much joy
Returning wounded soldiers, their stitches burst for joy.

PARTISANS

He hacks at a snowdrift:
She skims the pine needles
That drop into their soup,
Scattering on the snowcrust
Ideograms of 'peace'
And 'love', suchlike ideals.

BUCHENWALD MUSEUM

Among the unforgettable exhibits one
Was an official apology for bias. Outside

Although a snowfall had covered everything
A wreath of poppies was just about visible.

No matter how heavily the snow may come down
We have to allow the snow to wear a poppy.

THE FISHING PARTY

Because he loves off-duty policemen and their murderers
Christ is still seen walking on the water of Lough Neagh,
Whose fingers created bluebottles, meadow-browns, red
Admirals, painted ladies, fire-flies, and are tying now
Woodcock hackles around hooks, lamb's wool, badger fur

Until about his head swarm artificial flies and their names,
Dark Mackerel, Gravel Bed, Greenwell's Glory, Soldier
Palmer, Coachman, Water Cricket, Orange Grouse, Barm,
Without snagging in his hair or ceasing to circle above
Policemen turned by gunmen into fishermen for ever.

THE SCALES

Thick as the snowflakes on a wintry day when God
Comes down as snow and shows mankind his arsenal,
Putting the winds to sleep, blanketing in snowdrifts
Hill-tops, rocky promontories, pasture, turning
Jetties and beaches white, melting for breakers only –
So flew the stones, a snowstorm of stones, and then
A thunderstorm, shields crunching against shields,
Spears splintering, death-rattles, battle cries, dead-
Lock all morning, until God the Father at noon
Adjusted his golden scales, and in them weighed
Death sentences, holding the beam up by the middle
To see whose destiny would wobble heavenwards,
Whose come to rest on life-supporting earth, and whose
Faces, when God thundered, would go white as snow.

PHEMIOS & MEDON

Still looking for a scoot-hole, Phemios the poet
In swithers, fiddling with his harp, jukes to the hatch,
Lays the bruckle yoke between porringer and armchair,
Makes a ram-stam for Odysseus, grammels his knees,
Then bannies and bams wi this highfalutin blether:
'I ask for pity and respect. How could you condemn
A poet who writes for his people and Parnassus,
Autodidact, his repertoire god-given? I beg you
Not to be precipitate and cut off my head. Spare me
And I'll immortalise you in an ode. Telemachos
Your own dear son will vouch that I was no party-hack
At the suitors' dinner-parties. Overwhelmed and out-
Numbered, I gave poetry readings against my will.'
I gulder to me da: 'Dinnae gut him wi yer gully,
He's only a harmless crayter. And how's about Medon
The toast-master whose ashy-pet I was? Did ye ding him
When the oxherd and the swineherd stormed the steading?'
Thon oul gabble-blooter's a canny huer and hears me
From his fox's-slumber in cow-hides under a chair –
Out he spalters, flaffing his hands, blirting to my knees:
'Here I am, dear boy! Put in a word for me before
Your hot-blooded pater slaughters me as one of them –
The suitors I mean, bread-snappers, belly-bachelors.'
Long-headed Odysseus smiles at him and says: 'Wheesht!
You may thank Telemachos for this chance to wise up
And pass on the message of oul dacency. Go out
And sit in the haggard away from this massacre,
You and the well-spoken poet, while I redd the house.'
They hook it and hunker fornenst the altar of Zeus,
Afeard and skelly-eyed, keeking everywhere for death.

THE RULES OF BASEBALL

How long have we been hanging above the lights
   of O'Hare?
I reach beyond the wing and Chicago's skyline to Frank
And Mary's lopsided, laid-back, rickety, wooden home
Where we shall talk about poetry and the rules of baseball.
How many tons do we weigh in the cross-winds?
   Darkened
Seven-four-sevens are queueing up around the moon.

HOMER'S OCTOPUS

The poet may be dead and gone, but her/his
Poetry is like Homer's octopus
Yanked out of its hidey-hole, suckers
Full of tiny stones, except that the stones
Are precious stones or semi-precious stones.

CAVAFY'S DESIRES

Like corpses that the undertaker makes beautiful
And shuts, with tears, inside a costly mausoleum
– Roses at the forehead, jasmine at the feet – so
Desires look, after they have passed away
Unconsummated, without one night of passion
Or a morning when the moon stays in the sky.

SORESCU'S CIRCLES

With the three parts of water in my bones and tissues
Coloured blue; two eyes like sea-stars; my forehead
(The driest part) wrinkly, a carbon-copy of the earth's
Crust; my soul at sea making waves: have I the sense
To describe every day two circles – the merry-go-
Round around the sun and the roundabout of death?

THE PLEIADES

The moment I heard that Oisín Ferran had died in a fire
In his flat in Charlemont Street in Dublin, my mind
    became
The mind of the old woman who for ninety years
    had lived
In the middle of the Isle of Man and had never seen
The sea – and I helped him drag the smouldering mattress
Past the wash-basin and down the street and down
    the roads
That lead to the sea and my very first sight of the sea
And the sea put out the fire and washed his hands and face.

But when I knew that he was dead I found this memory
For Oisín of stars clustered on Inishbofin or Inishturk,
A farmstead out in the Atlantic, its kitchen door
Ajar while somebody turns on lights in the outhouses,
As though the sounds of pumps and buckets, boots
    and bolts
And safe animals – as though these sounds were visible
And had reached us from millions of miles away to sparkle
Like the Pleiades that rise out of the sea and set there.

HEADSTONE

I

The headstone for my parents' grave in Drumbo
    churchyard
I have imagined only: a triangular slab from the spiral
Staircase in the round tower that nearly overshadows
    them,
A stumpy ruin beside which I have seen myself standing
And following everyone's forefinger up into the sky.

II

Because he had survived in a coracle made out of feathers
I want to ask him about the lock-keeper's house at
    Newforge
Where a hole grows in the water, and about the towpath
That follows the Styx as far as the Minnowburn Beeches
And the end of his dream, and about the oars like wings.

III

As though her ashes had been its cargo when the
    ice-boat
Was rocked at dawn like a cradle and hauled from Shaw's
Bridge past Drumbo and Drumbeg, all the way
    to Aghalee,
I can hear in the frosty air above Acheron ice cracking
And the clatter of horses' hooves on the slippery towpath.

The wreck at Thallabaun whose timbers whistle in the
   wind
The tunes of shipwright, sawyer, cabinet-maker – adze
And axe and chisel following the grain – is my blue-print
For the ship of death, wood as hard as stone that keeps
Coming ashore with its cargo of sand and sandy water.

SUN & MOON

Could water take the weight of your illness ever,
Jonathan, in this story, say, about sun and moon
Who build a house with a garden big enough
For water to come and visit, but when water comes
With turtles and dolphins and fish, the garden
Overflows and then the house, floor by floor, until
Sun and moon climb out on to the roof to keep dry
And, finally, into the sky where they now live
And keep an eye on you in their underwater
House swimming through the doors and up the stairs?

WIND-FARMER

The wind-farmer's small-holding reaches as far as the
   horizon.
Between fields of hailstones and raindrops his frost-flowers
   grow.

BIRDSONG

'Where am I?' Consulting the *Modern School Atlas*
You underline Dalkey in Ireland, in Scotland Barrhead.
'What day is it?' Outside the home, house-sparrows
With precision tweetle and wheep under the eaves.

Although you forget their names, you hear the birds
In your own accent, the dawn chitter, evening chirl,
The woodpigeon's rooketty-coo and curdoo. 'Who
Am I? Where am I?' is what a bird might sing.

THE WHITE GARDEN

So white are the white flowers in the white garden that I
Disappear in no time at all among lace and veils.
For whom do I scribble the few words that come to me
From beyond the arch of white roses as from nowhere,
My memorandum to posterity? Listen. 'The saw
Is under the garden bench and the gate is unlatched.'

THE GHOST ORCHID

Added to its few remaining sites will be the stanza
I compose about leaves like flakes of skin, a colour
Dithering between pink and yellow, and then the root
That grows like coral among shadows and leaf-litter.
Just touching the petals bruises them into darkness.

CHINESE OCCASIONS

I

Snow piles up against the sunny window.
I burn my joss-sticks (a religious notion).
A blue tit tweetles from the patio.
The breeze sets a snowy twig in motion.

II

I am inspired by wind off the Lagan.
I tipple in the Black Mountain's shadow.
I fall into the flowerbed (drink taken),
Soil and sky my eiderdown and pillow.

III

They sip their whiskies on the patio.
Listen to them and what they listen to.
I close the door and open the window.
My friends grow feathers from top to toe.

IV

At the heart of the blue wisteria
A blackbird practises its aria.

RIVER & FOUNTAIN

I

I am walking backwards into the future like a Greek.
I have nothing to say. There is nothing I would describe.
It was always thus: as if snow has fallen on Front
Square, and, feeling the downy silence of the snowflakes
That cover cobbles and each other, white erasing white,
I read shadow and snow-drift under the Campanile.

II

'It fits on to the back of a postage stamp,' Robert said
As he scribbled out in tiny symbols the equation,
His silhouette a frost-flower on the window of my last
Year, his page the sky between chimney-stacks, his head
And my head at the city's centre aching for giddy
Limits, mathematics, poetry, squeaky nibs at all hours.

III

Top of the staircase, Number Sixteen in Botany Bay,
Slum-dwellers, we survived gas-rings that popped, slop-
Buckets in the bedrooms, changeable 'wives', and toasted
Doughy doorsteps, Freshmen turning into Sophisters
In front of the higgledy flames: our still-life, crusts
And buttery books, the half-empty marmalade jar.

My Dansette record player bottled up like genies
Sibelius, Shostakovich, Bruckner, dusty sleeves
Accumulating next to Liddel and Scott's *Greek–English*
Lexicon voices the fluffy needle set almost free.
I was the culture vulture from Ulster, Vincent's joke
Who heard *The Rite of Spring* and contemplated suicide.

V

Adam was first to read the maroon–covered notebooks
I filled with innocent outpourings, Adam the scholar
Whose stammer could stop him christening this and that,
Whose Eden was annotation and vocabulary lists
In a precise classicist's hand, the love of words as words.
My first and best review was Adam's 'I like these–I–I–'

V I

'College poet? Village idiot you mean!' (Vincent again).
In neither profession could I settle comfortably
Once Derek arrived reciting Rimbaud, giving names
To the constellations over the Examination Hall.
'Are you Longley? Can I borrow your typewriter? Soon?'
His was the first snow party I attended. I felt the cold.

VII

We were from the North, hitch-hikers on the Newry
    Road,
Faces that vanished from a hundred driving-mirrors
Down that warren of reflections – O'Neill's Bar,
    Nesbitt's –
And through Front Gate to Connemara and Inishere,
The raw experience of market towns and clachans, then
Back to Rooms, village of minds, poetry's townland.

VIII

Though College Square in Belfast and the Linen Hall
Had been our patch, nobody mentioned William Drennan.
In Dublin what dreams of liberty, the Index, the Ban:
Etonians on Commons cut our accents with a knife.
When Brendan from Ballylongford defied the Bishop, we
Flapped our wings together and were melted in the sun.

IX

A bath-house lotus-eater – fags, sodden *Irish Times* –
I tagged along with the Fabians, to embarrass Church
And State our grand design. Would-be class-warriors
We raised, for a moment, the Red Flag at the Rubrics,
Then joined the Civil Service and talked of Civil Rights.
Was Trinity a Trojan Horse? Were we Greeks at all?

X

'The Golden Mean is a tension, Ladies, Gentlemen,
And not a dead level': the Homeric head of Stanford
Who would nearly sing the first lines of the *Odyssey*.
That year I should have failed, but, teaching the *Poetics*,
He asked us for definitions, and accepted mine:
'Sir, if prose is a river, then poetry's a fountain.'

X I

Someone has skipped the seminar. Imagine his face,
The children's faces, my wife's: she sat beside me then
And they were waiting to be born, ghosts from a future
Without Tom: he fell in love just once and died of it.
Oh, to have turned away from everything to one face,
Eros and Thanatos your gods, icicle and dew.

X I I

Walking forwards into the past with more of an idea
I want to say to my friends of thirty years ago
And to daughters and a son that Belfast is our home,
Prose a river still – the Liffey, the Lagan – and poetry
A fountain that plays in an imaginary Front Square.
When snow falls it is feathers from the wings of Icarus.

THE OAR

I am meant to wander inland with a well-balanced oar
Until I meet people who know nothing about the sea
– Salty food, prows painted purple, oars that are ships'
Wings – and somebody mistakes the oar on my shoulder
For a winnowing fan:
                                    the signal to plant it in the ground
And start saying my prayers, to go on saying my prayers
Once I'm home, weary but well looked after in old age
By my family and friends and other happy islanders,
And death will come to me, a gentle sea-breeze, no more
        than
An exhalation, the waft from a winnowing fan or oar.

DUACH

I can be seen wherever I am standing, at my feet
Silverweed, five yellow petals surrounded by sand,
A sheep-path leading me on through a haze of hawkbit
To the burial mound that dwindles in my absence.

SANDPIPER

What does the sandpiper know of the river changing
    course,
The dry bed for her eggs that once was the otter's pool,
The heron's pool and the dragonflies', our pool as well
Where we made out of shoulders and shins our cataract?

SNOW BUNTING
for Sarah

At Allaran, the otters' rock, between the breakers'
Uninterrupted rummaging and – from the duach –
Larksong, I mistake your voice for your mother's voice
Deciphering otter prints long before you were born

As though you were conceived in a hayfield so small
Stone walls surrounded a single stook, and the snow
Bunting's putative tinkle from beyond the ridge
Sounded even closer than the spindrift's whispering.

OUT THERE

Do they ever meet out there,
The dolphins I counted,
The otter I wait for?
I should have spent my life
Listening to the waves.

NOTES & ACKNOWLEDGEMENTS

My version of the story of Baucis and Philemon (from Book VIII) was commissioned by Michael Hofmann and James Lasdun and published in *After Ovid: New Metamorphoses* (Faber). It gave rise to six other poems which are derived from, and in some cases combine, the stories of Arethusa, Cyane (Book V); Arachne (Book VI); Perdix (Book VIII); Pygmalion, Hyacinthus, the anemone (Book X); Phoenix (Book XV); and, lastly, from Ovid's account of the philosophy of Pythagoras (Book XV).

In seven poems I have combined free translations from Homer's *Iliad* and *Odyssey* with original lines. From the *Odyssey* the relevant passages are about Odysseus making himself a bed of leaves after nearly drowning (Book V); his sparing of Phemios and Medon (Book XXII); his anticipation of his own death (Books XI and XXIII): and, from the *Iliad*, Hector's farewell to Andromache (Book VI); the Trojan campfires (Book VIII); the scales of Zeus, and the snowstorm of stones (Book VIII); and Priam's visit to Achilles' camp to beg for the body of his son (Book XXIV).

'The Ship of the Wind' combines versions of 'Paradise Regained' by Hendrik Marsman and the first two stanzas of Karel van de Woestijne's 'The Oars Heavy with Seaweed', two of several poems which I translated in collaboration with Peter van de Kamp for his anthology *Turning Tides: Modern Dutch and Flemish Verse in English Versions by Irish Poets* (Story Line Press). 'Sorescu's Circles' compresses phrases from my version of 'Map' which was included in a collection of translations of Marin Sorescu's poems, *The Biggest Egg in the World* (Bloodaxe Books).

I have also borrowed from Virgil's *Third Georgic*, Horace's *Ars Poetica* and the *Penguin Book of Chinese Verse* translated by Robert Kotewall and Norman L. Smith and edited by A.R. Davis (Penguin Books).

'River & Fountain' was commissioned by Trinity College Dublin as part of the Quatercentenary commemorations and read on Friday, 13 March 1992, in the Public Theatre at the ceremony to mark the College's Charter Day.

'Sitting for Eddie' was written specially for *Edward McGuire*, Brian Fallon's study of the painter (Irish Academic Press).

'Baucis & Philemon', with drawings by James Allen, was published as a pamphlet by Poet & Printer. Seven of the shorter poems appeared in Morning Star Folio 5/1, *Birds and Flowers*, with a watermark of the ghost orchid created by Raymond Piper and Gary Hincks.

'Behind a Cloud', 'Cavafy's Desires', 'A Flowering', 'Snow-hole' and 'Spiderwoman' first appeared in the *New Yorker*.

Acknowledgements are also due to the editors of the *Belfast News Letter*, *Edinburgh Review*, *Force Ten*, *Fortnight*, *Icarus*, *Independent on Sunday*, *Irish Review*, *Irish Times*, *Krino*, *London Review of Books*, *New Writing 2*, *Observer*, *Poetry Book Society Anthology 3*, *Poetry Review*, *Soho Square*, *Southern Review*, *Threepenny Review*, *Times Literary Supplement*, *Verse*, *Yale Review*; and to the BBC and Radio Telefis Eireann.

Love poems, elegies: I am losing my place.
Elegies come between me and your face.